RULES FOR REVERENDS

Text copyright © Jeremy Fletcher 2013
Illustrations copyright © Dave Walker 2013
The author asserts the moral right to be identified as the author of this work

Published by
The Bible Reading Fellowship
15 The Chambers, Vineyard
Abingdon OX14 3FE
United Kingdom
Tel: +44 (0)1865 319700
Email: enquiries@brf.org.uk
Website: www.brf.org.uk
BRF is a Registered Charity

ISBN 978 1 84101 657 3

First published 2013
10 9 8 7 6 5 4 3 2 1 0

A catalogue record for this book is available from the British Library

Printed in the UK by MWL

RULES FOR REVERENDS

Jeremy Fletcher

Illustrated by Dave Walker

CONTENTS

THE BEGINNING

I spent the 'noughties' not being a parish priest. After being a bishop's chaplain and then working in a cathedral, I returned to general parish work, and things I'd learnt ten years before started to come back to me.

One evening last winter, I was looking for a house to do a baptism visit. It hit me: the rule was that, because it was dark, the one I was looking for would be the only one without an obvious number. When I did find it, I just knew that its doorbell wouldn't work.

When I got home, I wrote those 'rules' down. More came very quickly, and I put them on my blog (http://jeremyfletcher. wordpress.com). People seemed to recognise them. I wrote some more—and here's the result.

Clergy inhabit a fantastic, pressurised, privileged, frustrating and humbling role. These 'rules' are dedicated to the ordained and, indeed, anyone who does anything like the job of a parish priest. I have shamelessly stolen some of this material from you. You know who you are. (Good job, because I've forgotten.)

What follows is not serious, really. Except when it is. You'll have to decide.

All Saints Stranton, St Nicholas' Nottingham, St Andrew's Skegby, All Saints' Stanton Hill, St Katherine's Teversal, the

Diocese of Southwell, York Minster, Beverley Minster, St Leonard's Molescroft, St Peter's Woodmansey, the Church in Tickton, All Saints' Routh… none of this book is about you, obviously.

My family have lived this job with me for a quarter of a century, and deserve far more thanks than I can give. At least I've not mentioned them too much in sermons…

GENERAL STUFF

Because life isn't as compartmentalised as you might like

The only people who ring before 9 o'clock in the morning are undertakers. Or bishops.

In a PCC meeting, even those you know well will say stuff that you wouldn't believe.

The one time you answer the phone in an amusing way will be the one time you wish you hadn't.

Just because you're on Twitter, it doesn't make you acceptable to the young.

Everything stops in September. You thought that's when it started, but that's when your congregation (who are all retired) go on cruises.

Falling asleep during a clergy quiet day isn't a sin, but it's embarrassing if you dribble.

Annual Parochial Church Meetings would be enlivened if people could be voted off rather than on. But you might be first.

The press has the memory of a goldfish, and works on whims and timescales more rapid than a toddler in a toyshop. You will not change this.

Some people will never ever be satisfied. Find out who they are, and spend as little time as possible trying to sort things out for them.

People who light a candle when they say a prayer are not being superstitious. The Holy Spirit is helping them with sighs too deep for words.

No church hall booking system ever works properly.

No, the Diocese does not know what it is doing.

If you want something to thrive, threaten to abolish it.

Always accept a resignation.

If you can't be omniscient, you can give the impression of being omnipresent. And you don't have to stay to the end.

If the whole team is last minute, you'll get on well with each other and your church will learn what faith is all about.

No one is ever happy about car parking arrangements. For any event. Anywhere.

Work out how you respond best to conflict, because there will be some. The Body of Christ is made up of human beings, after all. And the Holy Spirit doesn't make it easier. Look at Corinth.

The preferred communication style of most churches is osmosis and telepathy.

Look carefully at the retired clergypeople around you. Find a happy one, and ask them how they did it. Start planning to do the same. You could be retired a long time.

Loud shoes in stone-floored churches are much to be encouraged.

There might be loads of clergy at the cathedral, but they do work hard. It's just different from what you do.

Being on the committee of another organisation is a good way of realising that perhaps the PCC isn't so bad after all. Or recognising that, actually, it is.

The contents of the flower cupboard are a mystery, one not to be explored without prayer and fasting.

Answering machines are superb, but you do need to listen to them.

Gardening is only therapeutic when your parishioners can't see you doing it. When they do, they think you're taking too much time off.

If you need a decent policy for something, ask your friendly Methodists. They've got loads of good ones.

There is no such thing as a quiet toy.

Never doubt the power of a nun to get conversations going. Especially on public transport.

Fill in attendance numbers carefully, and review them year by year. Some trends take time to make themselves felt.

Working harder at this job won't get you any more money. Unless you become a bishop, a dean or an archdeacon. And who wants to be one of them?

If you get a lone bagpiper to play a lament, have plenty of hankies handy.

Most church problems are sorted out by the people who know, in the car park afterwards. It's not worth having the original meeting at all, when you think about it.

If you have the NRSV on your smartphone, you can update your Facebook profile during worship and pretend you're reading the Bible.

Visitations are only made by angels, archdeacons and the Blessed Virgin Mary. Not all Visitations are the same.

At least with Alpha you get food.

When you talk with children, do it on their level. Physically, too. And listen.

There is always something you wish they'd taught you in training, and something else you wish they'd left until you were ordained.

It's interesting how the words 'swearing' and 'churchwardens' go together.

No one understands what a stipend is or what it's worth. Least of all you.

Lots of stuff in your job is the same as other people's jobs. Try to remember what's unique to your calling—and make time to do it. Praying for your people is a good start.

How Christian it is of people to share their coughs and sneezes by bringing them to church.

Deanery Synods... conclusive proof of the truth of the doctrine of Limbo.

There will come a point in your life when you hear yourself saying 'Amen' loudly at the end of someone else's prayer a good two seconds before everyone else. This is what older clergy do. You used to hate it.

Rural Deans… not rural, not deans.

If you do the washing-up, at least you'll start with a mess and end with it sorted out. Nothing else in your day will be like this.

By all means type out emails last thing at night. Just don't send them until the next morning.

Beware the vicar who has just returned from the Holy Land.

If you have a finely developed taste in music and literature, you'll need to put it on hold on more occasions than you might think.

For 95 per cent of the congregation, what you know to be part of a wonderfully crafted and theologically satisfying sermon series is just what you happen to be preaching about on the day when they turn up.

Never take your diary with you to church.

Have fun with the last appointments you make before you leave. Your successor will love you for it.

If you have three or more churches, you will, at least once a year, design a rota that requires you to bi-locate. Not even you can do this.

If you let the children of the choir/Sunday school at the biscuits first, there will be none left for anyone else. Devise a plan to avoid this. Or frighten the children out of church all together. That will not be difficult.

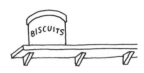

The bulk of your thinking time should be spent working out exciting names for your existing activities, to make them more attractive.

If you don't want people to ring you on routine matters after 9pm, don't do the same to them.

Some people can only survive if they are complaining. Why not complain back and see what happens?

Beware of doing the same thing three times. The view will then be that you've always done it, and you will be reported to the bishop if you stop. Even if it was your idea in the first place.

Make sure you:

- have a regular day off, and an extra day off every now and again

- take your full complement of holidays

- have a retreat and regular quiet days

- attend a range of courses for your CME

- go to conferences and teaching days in the wider church

- attend the days your bishop calls you to

- go faithfully to every meeting of Chapter and the Deanery Synod

- do some further study to keep your theological faculties sharp

- have a hobby

In the one day left to you after all this in a typical year, you can do your pastoral work as well.

WORSHIP

The person who looks most miserable in a special service will be the one who tells you at the end how much they loved it.

No, the compilers of the Lectionary didn't know what they were doing.

There should be a misprint in every order of service. Only God is perfect.

Vergers (or Virgers) are God's way of saying, 'I love you.'

Some people have very noisy coats.

Services are better when planned with other people. Your week will be better if you don't have so many meetings. In the middle of this tension, God is to be found.

You drink more Communion wine than anyone else. You owe it to yourself to make it decent.

The tiptoeing thing people do when they're late into church doesn't work.

Common Worship was written so that people previously at enmity with each other could have something to moan about together.

Yes, it's frustrating not to be able to join in at Choral Evensong. Just let go, and let the office pray you.

In a procession, you will feel an idiot when you turn a corner at right angles. But it will look wonderful.

You are allowed to smile at people if you're in a procession. Stopping to pose for photos is best left to Roman Catholic bishops. Bless babies only if you are an archbishop.

If you receive any more than three standards at the beginning of a military service, you will inevitably give them out in the wrong order at the end.

It's no use just having a clip-mic on. It does need to be somewhere near your mouth. And pointing towards it, too.

A large congregation turning a page makes the sound of many waters.

It's generally when you just want to get through it and get home that God turns up.

In any worship event you are not leading, you will be both receiving stuff and wondering how you would do it if you were the leader.

The [insert name of annual event] Service happens once a year. Do you really want to create more work for the Holy Spirit by choosing new hymns? Use last year's.

Just because it says 'Please sit' in the Order of Service, that doesn't mean a thing.

Other people's Pet Services look like such a good idea, don't they? But yours will be the one where the snake escapes.

Wars have been fought over the right way to announce a hymn.

Incense and fire detection systems don't mix.

Singers: mouth open; look at the conductor. The rest is detail.

You will receive your first complaint about a service you thought was brilliant within ten minutes of arriving home.

Choristers: always follow the person in front of you in a procession. Never be at the front of a procession.

Choristers have to work very hard to make sure they have the right stuff to sing at the right time. They might not, therefore, take in what else is happening in your brilliantly crafted act of worship. Give them some input another way.

No one will notice if the vicar does their bit at the wrong time. Everyone will notice when the organist does. Cut them some slack.

Organists are uniformly lovely, and uniformly misunderstood.

There is a 'right' tune for every hymn. It's just rarely the one you chose.

Never smile at the choir. It only encourages them.

Most people's worst nightmare is a vicar with a guitar. This situation is helpfully relieved by saying, 'I know. I am your worst nightmare—a vicar with a guitar.' When tuning up, give them a bit of 'All right now' (Free) or 'Thunderstruck' (AC/DC). It works for me.

If your worship group has a drummer, pray that they are the most musical person in the building.

All hymns/songs that make it into the second edition of a hymn/song book are obviously divinely inspired, and their music and words must not be changed under any circumstances.

In heaven you will probably meet the person who invented the tambourine. You can look forward to this. Unless they're somewhere else.

LENT, HOLY WEEK AND EASTER

Make your ash in good time. It hurts if it's hot.

Palm crosses are flame-retardant. If you're going to burn them, you need to warm them first.

It's weird to get Lent sorted in early autumn. But it will feel good if you do.

People who hate groups will join one in Lent.

Giving up going to church is not an option. For you, at least.

Do not overestimate the power of daffodils on Mothering Sunday.

Big nails. Worth a thousand words on Good Friday.

Hot cross buns. Well, it's a Christian duty.

The more you tell people that the Easter egg is like the stone rolled away from the tomb, the less you'll believe it.

If you eat a daffodil as an illustration ('Did you believe what you just saw? Would anyone believe you if you told them?') just make sure that you (a) wash it first; (b) only eat the petals, not the stem. Trust me.

Of course the resurrection is just as true on the Second Sunday of Easter. It just won't feel like it.

It's actually quite hard to preach about Jesus not being here. Even though he is—but not in that way.

CHRISTMAS

Christmas happens on 25 December every year. It is amazing the number of times you will not realise this until it's too late.

On paper, carol services look as if they're going to be really long, but they are shorter than you think.

Increased attendances at your Christmas services may well be to do with the effectiveness of your ministry throughout the year. Or it could just be that it's the weekend and the weather is mild.

The person who thought that an orange, some ribbon, sweets and a candle would be an aid to worship had to be joking. No one's laughing now.

You might have sung 'Hark the herald' 13 times already, but for most of the congregation it's their only time in church this year.

You might have more of an effect by just being nice to people at Christmas rather than seizing the annual opportunity to hammer them with your best evangelistic sermon.

The Crib Service… instant church growth.

CRIB
SERVICE
THIS AFTERNOON

BRING A
NATIVITY FIGURE

CLERGY HOUSEHOLDS

However hard they try not to, your ordained parent will mention you in a sermon.

You will try various combinations of how to do family presents and Christmas services. None of them will work.

Your dog will be badly behaved. This is essential.

What is the point of growing up in a vicarage and not having elaborate funerals for your pets, complete with gravestones?

You live in a large house because you are supposed to exercise hospitality. But you don't get paid enough to heat it or to buy the kind of food you can be hospitable with… unless your spouse goes out to work… and then you're too tired to be hospitable. Good, isn't it?

You're not supposed to turn a job down because of the house.
But some houses are just stupid.

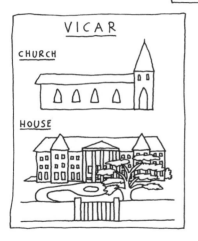

MONEY

Take great care over finances, and learn to read a balance sheet. The level of giving is a barometer of the spiritual life of the congregation.

Never handle any cash. If you have to, get a witness.

People are very coy and very careful about their giving.
Be coy and careful back, but make sure they know they are
appreciated.

The length of a PCC discussion about finance will be in
inverse proportion to the amount of money being discussed.

Account very carefully for special collections, and write within nanoseconds to the donor and recipient.

Pray very hard that your treasurer is the person in your congregation closest to God.

CURATES

An interregnum is good for you. So is a vicar's sabbatical.
A few years after the event, you will know this to be true.

If you're having a lovely time in your curacy, there will be
plenty of others in your diocese who aren't. Gloating is
probably something to keep to yourself.

Of course your curate is better than you at stuff. Get over it.

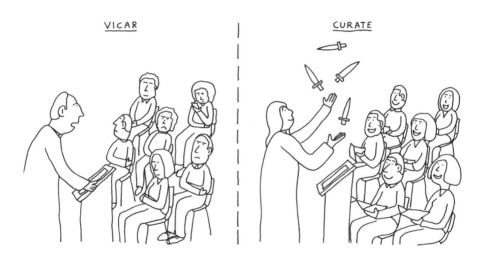

Of course your vicar is wrong. Get over it.

You are taking your first funeral. You are nervous. But you know more about what to do than the congregation does.

Supervision… God's sanctification of gossip.

Training incumbents console themselves that doing things badly at least gives their curates something to react against.

SOCIAL EVENTS

No jug or teapot in church should pour properly. This is a law.

Declaring that raffles and tombolas are the same as gambling and should be banned is just cheating.

You may not be designed for small talk. Watch a master, and steal three phrases which will help. Asking people about themselves is a good starter.

Under no circumstances agree to judge a fancy dress competition where there is any possibility of meeting any contestant, or any member of their family, during their lifetime.

Some different-coloured raffle tickets are hard to tell apart.

The law of buffets is that the optimum arrangement of food and plates has not yet been discovered, and that all the other ones are achingly slow.

What they don't teach you at theological college is how to hold a plate and a glass of wine and a fork at the same time. They really should.

Learn how to call a raffle quickly. Otherwise there will be many, many hours of your life that you will never get back.

If cups and saucers are provided, they must be green. This is another law.

BISHOPS

You can always tell a bishop, but you can't tell him much.

When you go to see the bishop about your future, bear in mind that he might have said his prayers that morning. But then again, he might just have a gap to fill.

You only have to obey the bishop 'in all things lawful and honest'.

Bishops who can read in the car get more things done. As long as they are not driving at the time.

Get someone to tell you whether purple is your colour. You don't have to wear it.

If flying bishops could actually fly, they wouldn't spend so much time in the car.

Absolutely no bishop anywhere has ever looked good wearing a mitre.

Bishops must announce their retirements many months in advance. This is to allow the diocese to save up for a nice present.

No surprise is more pleasant than a letter from the bishop by return.

SCHOOLS

No Year 1 assembly will survive if you mention the word 'Christmas'.

It's not so bad being a school governor. But the meetings are all at times that require you to miss your tea.

It is an odd feeling when OFSTED come to your collective worship.

You will get no reaction at all when you take a secondary school assembly. But they will be laughing inside.

Work out how the schools in your patch can all come to your church(es). They will want to.

WHAT (NOT) TO WEAR

Never be afraid to admit that part of you is in it for the dressing-up.

Every vicar's surplice has a darker patch where it's been slammed into a funeral director's car door.

You think that wearing a dog collar will get you a better deal or add weight when you complain. It won't.

The real clergy who model for clerical dress catalogues must be desperate for cash. And they don't look real anyway.

If you buy a thick cassock because all churches are cold, you will only ever work in warm ones.

There is probably a way of remembering which of your robes is in which of your churches or in your house. If you've discovered it, please let the rest of us know.

When walking about wearing a dog collar, have a smile ready for people who look at you. But beware of smiling at strangers when you've forgotten you're not wearing it. You'll just look creepy.

Never cross your legs in a cassock.

Aggressive gestures at other drivers are given added spice when you are fully robed.

You don't have to make an emergency dog collar any more if you've forgotten the real one. Just say you agree with Archbishop Sentamu's stand on these things.

Black clerical shirts eventually go green. It's worth checking occasionally.

Think very carefully before trusting anyone wearing a pectoral cross who is not a bishop.

Old cassocks never die. They just smell that way.

There is never a pen in your cassock pocket—even when you know you left one there the last time you had it on.

WEDDINGS

You are not there to outshine the bride, nor to give the best man's speech.

There is nothing so very wrong with wedding photographers. When there is, do give them some feedback.

You might think you've got loads of weddings. You have fewer than there were 30 years ago. Why not try to get some more?

There might just be florists in heaven. Miracles do happen.

Banns of marriage might be an antiquated thing. But couples like to hear them, and that means new people in church. Don't waste the opportunity.

If all your notices are about what people mustn't do, you'll just sound grumpy. This may, of course, be the effect you are trying to achieve.

'Please remember to switch your mobile phone back on at the end of the service' is a neat way to do it.

A sensitively taken photo during the service might just be a permanent reminder of their profound moment before God. Is a click at that point so very bad?

If you hold a wedding fair, be sure to include the Mothers' Union. Placing them next to the 'cosmetic procedures' stall is optional.

PEOPLE

The house you are looking for in the dark will be the one without a number.

No doorbell ever works.

Do not trust any dog that 'just wants to play'.

Being more interested in the parents' Mercedes/motorbike/
hi-fi than in their baby is not good form on a baptism visit.

People who say they are sorry for disturbing you because you're very busy really mean it, and really are.

No other role gets you involved in the highest and lowest points of people's lives, especially not all in the same afternoon.

Visiting on spec is a waste of time because no one is ever in during the day. Except for the people who are.

People have long memories, and everyone is related to everyone else. Be careful.

Each one of your parishioners is made in God's image. You just need to look harder at some of them.

Hardly anyone will refuse if you offer to pray for them.

Sending a text at the right time can be a deeply pastoral act.

You can't help watching someone's TV, even with the sound turned down.

There is absolutely no way you can look at your watch when in a deep pastoral situation without the other person noticing.

Saying 'Yes please' when offered a drink in someone's home is an extreme sport.

If your church has lots of needy people, it's probably because it's doing the right thing. But that doesn't make it easier to handle.

The person at your door asking for money and food might be a prophet. But they just might be dangerous and frightening to your family and you have to be careful.

By all means answer your mobile phone while in the middle of a one-to-one conversation. The person you're with won't mind.

Have a clock that you can look at without making it obvious, in the place where you see people. In other people's houses, the clocks on their electrical equipment are very useful.

Vicars who keep up-to-date notes about every pastoral encounter are only one stage away from sainthood. You are many stages away, so learn how to bluff while you struggle to remember stuff.

The people who get most annoyed that the vicar doesn't visit are not the ones in need of a visit, but those who think that other people need one.

You need a very secure safe for all the special things people
entrust you with.

If people are having a hard time, it's best not to try to explain
it theologically. Just be with them, and pray as if you were
them.

FUNERALS

Families divided in life can be even more divided in death. You may have to be a peacekeeper during the funeral visit.

No music chosen by a family is inappropriate at a funeral.

You don't necessarily have to say anything when you sit with someone who is dying. It's a privilege just to be there.

Return an undertaker's call immediately. Some things can't wait.

There is something curiously uplifting about doing 70mph in a hearse.

Crematoria… nicer places than you'd think.

Maintain a dignified expression during 'Always look on the bright side of life'. Joining in with it does not play well.

It's amazing how many God-fearing good people you will bury who have never been to church. Someone should probably do a PhD on this.

What do funeral directors do in heaven? Sit at a desk and take complaints.

If someone else does a tribute, tell them to write it down and remind them that it's roughly 100 words a minute. And ask to see a copy.

The most emotional funeral visit is the one you're not expecting to be.

Keep all your notes from funerals, and throw none away. They are useful years later.

PREACHING

Always have a grace ready. Or 'a few words'. Or (in Africa) a sermon.

It is impossible to overestimate the impact on your ministry of using clear consonants and not dropping your voice at the end of a sentence.

Just because the microphone is there, it doesn't mean everyone will automatically hear you.

It's only when you're in the pulpit and coughing that you realise you're not sure whether the jug and glass have been there for five years without being changed.

Switch off your microphone before you blow your nose.

The recycled sermon you use in desperation will be the only one someone remembers from the first time.

Two questions that your congregation should be able to answer after you've preached: 'So what?' and 'What now?'

BUILDINGS

People who have worshipped in the same church for decades have rarely looked around it properly. Preach about the windows or a carving. They will be amazed.

The best way of galvanising the 99 per cent of your parish who never come to church is to promise to remove a pew.

If you can't find it, look under the altar.

There will be one key that unlocks the drawer that has all the other keys to the building and safes in it. This key will be in plain sight somewhere.

Buildings are historical. Congregations are contemporary. The gap between is filled with form-filling... and the members of the congregation who are historical.

There is nothing more dated than a contemporary building.

The DAC is your friend, and the Faculty process will save your life.

All pews are sacred.

Fitted carpet bad. Rugs good.

You don't notice your noticeboard any more. But other people will.

Decide which practical things in your church you will know nothing about. They could be how the clock is wound or the way the boiler works. You do not have to do everything, only the stuff you have to do. Discovering what this is will be your life's work.

Diocesan Chancellors never die. They just lose their faculties.

You were ordained so that you could use the word 'quinquennial' more than once every five years. That makes it all worthwhile.

Putting a memorial inscription on something like a chair will make it very difficult to get rid of in a few decades' time.

ORGANISATIONS

Some organisations do die. Give them an honourable and joyful funeral.

The Mothers' Union might just surprise you.

Don't mess with the flower arrangers.

A remarkable number of people have been Cubs or Brownies at some point. Give your uniformed organisations some attention.

There are more missionary societies and good causes than you can ever pray for or support. You'll just have to choose.

Young Mums… probably not young any more.

Soroptimists… the special forces of women's organisations.

You can learn a lot from watching your bell ringers in action. But don't even try to understand what a Stedman Triple is.

THE END

Who else can pronounce a blessing on people and say it's work?

No, it's not a job. Yes, it is the best in the world.

Enjoyed this book?

Write a review—we'd love to hear what you think. Email: reviews@brf.org.uk

Sign up for email news and select your interest groups at: www.brfonline.org.uk/findoutmore/

Follow us on Twitter @brfonline

To receive new title information by post (UK only), complete the form below and post to:
BRF Mailing Lists, 15 The Chambers, Vineyard, Abingdon, Oxfordshire, OX14 3FE

Name _____	
Address_____	
_____ Post Code _____	
Email_____	

Your Interest Groups (*Please tick as appropriate)

☐ Advent/Lent   ☐ Messy Church
☐ Bible Reading & Study   ☐ Pastoral
☐ Children's Books   ☐ Prayer & Spirituality
☐ Discipleship   ☐ Resources for Children's Church
☐ Leadership   ☐ Resources for Schools